HOW TO MASTER MAKING CHOCOLATE MOUSSE AND SOUFFLÉS

BY

MEALLÁ H FALLON

Copyright © 2013 Meallá H Fallon
All rights reserved.

Second Edition 2018

ISBN-13:978-1497479531
ISBN-10:1497479533

TABLE OF CONTENTS

Mastering Chocolate Mousse and Soufflés 2
Chocolate Mousse 3
   Basic Dark Chocolate Mousse Recipe 4
   Basic White Chocolate Mousse Recipe 6
   Blueberry Chocolate Mousse In Sugar Cone Bowls 10
   Cardamom Orange Chocolate Mousse In Brandy Glasses 13
   Chocolate Mousse Layered Oreo Cookies In Large Glass Bowl 15
   Dark Chocolate Cherry Mousse In Filo Nests 17
   Double Chocolate Mousse Cake 20
   Irish Coffee Chocolate Mousse 23
   Kahlua Chocolate Mousse In Chocolate Shot Glasses 25
   Peppermint Chocolate Mousse In Shot Glasses 28
   Triple Chocolate Mousse Mini Cakes 30

White Chocolate Mousse In Chocolate Sugar Cone Bowls 34
White Chocolate Mousse In Dark Chocolate Bowls 37
Dessert Soufflés 42
Chocolate Soufflé Recipe 44
Chocolate Raspberry Soufflé 47
Lemon Soufflé 50
Lime And Coconut Soufflé 53
Mocha Soufflé 56
Rose Soufflé 58
Vanilla Soufflé 61

Mastering Chocolate Mousse and Soufflés

Chocolate mousse and sweet soufflés – they seem to be so exotic and difficult to make BUT they are not!!!!

In this book I will show you how to make these 2 exotic looking desserts without much effort. The presentation is the key, you can make the mousse or soufflé look way more complicated by the way you present and serve it.

Chocolate Mousse

Here Are 2 Basic Chocolate Mousse Recipes:

- Dark chocolate mousse
- White chocolate mousse

These 2 recipes can be changed to create all the different chocolate mousse variations and ideas that this book offers.

Basic Dark Chocolate Mousse Recipe

NOTE:

Before you start making the basic recipe first check on the section - Different Variations On Serving The Chocolate Mousse – there are ingredients that need to be added or substituted depending on the variation of chocolate mousse you want to make.

Also use the best quality chocolate you can afford. It does make a difference to the chocolate mousse.

Ingredients

- 600 g dark chocolate (get the best quality chocolate you can afford)
- 50 ml brandy
- 40 g butter
- 4 eggs (separated)
- 400 ml cream (whipped)

Method

Break the chocolate into small even pieces.

Combine the chocolate, butter and egg yolks together in the top of a double boiler.

Stir until the mixture has melted.

Remove from the heat.

Allow the mixture to cool.

Add the brandy.

Whisk the egg whites until stiff.

Gently fold the egg whites, chocolate mixture and whipped cream together.

Now you are ready to follow one of the serving suggestions – see section "Different Variations On Serving The Chocolate Mousse".

Basic White Chocolate Mousse Recipe

NOTE:

Before you start making the basic recipe first check on the section - Different Variations On Serving The Chocolate Mousse – there are ingredients that need to be added or substituted depending on the variation of chocolate mousse you want to make.

Also use the best quality chocolate you can afford. It does make a difference to the chocolate mousse.

Ingredients

- 200 g white chocolate (get the best quality chocolate you can buy)
- 120 ml milk
- 30 g gelatin
- 120 ml evaporated milk
- 2 egg yolks (beaten)

4 egg whites

100 g sugar

10 ml vanilla extract

400 ml double cream (whipped until stiff)

Method

Break the chocolate into small even pieces.

Combine the white chocolate and evaporated milk together in the top of a double boiler.

Stir until the mixture has melted.

Remove from the heat.

Allow the mixture to cool.

Combine the gelatin and evaporated milk together.

Leave the gelatin mixture for 5 minutes.

Microwave the gelatin mixture for 40 seconds.

Combine the melted chocolate mixture, egg yolks and gelatin mixture together.

Cool the mixture over ice water.

Whisk the egg whites until frothy.

Add the sugar and vanilla extract very gradually.

Whisk until stiff peaks form.

Fold the chocolate mixture, egg whites and cream together.

Now you are ready to follow one of the serving suggestions – see section "Different Variations On Serving The Chocolate Mousse".

DIFFERENT VARIATIONS ON SERVING THE CHOCOLATE MOUSSE

Blueberry Chocolate Mousse In Sugar Cone Bowls

Serve the Blueberry Chocolate Mousse In Sugar Cone Bowls – 1 per guest. This mousse recipe serves 4 servings.

Ingredients

- 2 egg whites
- 375 ml sugar
- 250 ml flour
- 50 ml butter (melted)
- 10 ml vanilla extract
- 125 ml milk
- 1 mixture of Basic White Chocolate Mousse
- 10 ml blueberry extract – substitute for the vanilla extract
- Blueberries for serving
- Whipped cream for decorating (spoon into a piping bag with a rosette nozzle)

Method

Whisk the egg whites until soft peaks are formed.

Beat in the sugar gradually.

Whisk the egg whites until they are stiff.

Add the flour, butter, milk and vanilla extract to the egg white mixture.

Mix well.

Line a baking sheet with parchment paper.

Draw 2 circles on the parchment paper.

Drop 37,5 ml batter into the centre of each circle.

Spread the batter to edges of the circles.

Bake the circles at 400 degrees F for 6 to 8 minutes.

Place the baked circles Bottom Side up on a paper towel.

Pull off the parchment paper.

Invert small bowls to use as molds.

Place the hot baked circles directly over the bottoms of the bowls.

The circles will harden as they cool.

When the sugar bowls have cooled enough to handle carefully remove them from the bowls.

Make the White Chocolate Mousse – replace the vanilla extract with blueberry extract.

Just before serving spoon the white chocolate mousse into the sugar cone bowls.

Spoon the blueberries on top of the white chocolate mousse.

Pipe rosettes of whipped cream on top of the blueberries and white chocolate mousse.

Cardamom Orange Chocolate Mousse In Brandy Glasses

Serve the Cardamom Orange Chocolate Mousse in brandy glasses – 1 per guest. This mousse recipe serves 4 servings.

Ingredients

- 1 mixture of Basic Dark Chocolate Mousse
- 50 ml Orange Liqueur or orange juice – substitution for brandy
- 5 ml ground cardamom
- 10 ml orange zest
- Whipped cream for decorating (spoon into a piping bag with a rosette nozzle)
- Candied orange slices for decorating

Method

Make the Dark Chocolate Mousse – use Orange liqueur or orange juice instead of brandy.

Add cardamom and orange zest to the mousse.

Spoon the mousse into a piping bag with a rosette nozzle.

Pipe the mousse into the brandy glasses in a spiral.

Ball Shaped Brandy Glass

Pipe rosettes of whipped cream on top of the chocolate mousse.

Decorate with candied orange slices.

Chocolate Mousse Layered Oreo Cookies In Large Glass Bowl

This chocolate mousse gets made in one a large glass container.

Ingredients

- 1 mixture of Basic Dark Chocolate Mousse
- 50 ml Cherry liqueur – substitute for brandy
- Whipped cream
- Oreo cookies – broken into pieces
- Maraschino cherries
- Whipped cream for decorating (spoon into a piping bag with a rosette nozzle)
- Maraschino cherries and chocolate curls to decorate

Method

Make the Dark Chocolate Mousse – replace the brandy with Cherry liqueur.

The Dark Chocolate Mousse, Oreo cookie pieces and Maraschino cherries should be layered in the glass bowl.

Glass Serving Bowl

Make at least 3 layers of each - Chocolate Mousse, Oreo cookie pieces and Maraschino cherries.

Now pipe a layer of whipped cream on top of the chocolate mousse and cookie layers.

Decorate with Maraschino cherries and chocolate curls.

Dark Chocolate Cherry Mousse In Filo Nests

Serve the Dark Chocolate Cherry Mousse in Filo Nests – 1 per guest. This mousse recipe serves 4 servings.

Ingredients

Filo pastry
1 mixture of Basic Dark Chocolate Mousse
50 ml Cherry Liqueur – substitution for brandy
Maraschino cherries
Chocolate curls to decorate

Method

Pre-heat the oven to 190 degrees C.

Invert 6 metal dariole molds onto a baking sheet.

Cut the Filo pastry into 16 rectangles.

Drape a rectangle of Filo pastry over the dariole mold.

Place another piece of Filo pastry at right angles to the first piece.

Pinch the pastry into frills at the bottom.

Criss-cross with 2 more pieces of Filo pastry.

Pinch the pastry into frills at the bottom.

Repeat this process for the other 5 dariole molds.

Bake at 190 degrees C for 10 minutes.

Remove from the oven and cool slightly.

Remove the "nests" off the dariole molds.

Allow the Filo pastry nests to cool.

Now make the Dark Chocolate Mousse – use Cherry liqueur instead of brandy.

Just before serving spoon the Dark Chocolate Mousse into the Filo nests.

Arrange the Maraschino cherries on top of the mousse.

Decorate the Filo nests with the chocolate curls.

Dariole Mold

Double Chocolate Mousse Cake

Slice the mousse cake and serve on a dessert plate (stand the slice upright) – a slice per guest.

Ingredients

400 g chocolate cookies (crushed)
75 ml butter (melted)
1 mixture of Basic Dark Chocolate Mousse
1 mixture of Basic White Chocolate Mousse
Dark chocolate (melted) for decorating
Pecans (chopped) for decorating
Icing sugar to dust sliced mousse cake

Method

Combine the chocolate cookies and melted butter together. Mix well.

Press the cookie mixture into the bottom of a greased spring-form pan (do not press the cookie crumbs around the sides of the pan).

Spring-form Pan

Refrigerate the cookie base for 10 minutes or until needed.

Now make the Dark Chocolate Mousse and White Chocolate Mousse – no variations are required to the basic recipes.

Spoon the Dark Chocolate Mousse into the spring-form pan on top of the cookie layer.

Make sure the layer is level and smooth on top.

Gently spoon the White Chocolate Mousse on top of the Dark Chocolate Mousse layer.

Make sure the layer is level and smooth on top.

Refrigerate the mousse cake for at least 6 hours to make sure it has set (preferably overnight).

Just before serving remove the chocolate mousse cake from the spring-form pan.

Drizzle the melted dark chocolate over the top and sides of the chocolate mousse cake.

Sprinkle with the chopped pecans while the drizzled chocolate is still wet.

Slice the mousse cake and serve on a dessert plate (stand the slice upright) – a slice per guest.

Dust the slices of mousse cake with icing sugar just before serving.

Irish Coffee Chocolate Mousse

Serve Irish Coffee Chocolate Mousse – 1 per guest.

Ingredients

1 mixture of Basic Dark Chocolate Mousse
50 ml Whiskey – substitute for the brandy
5 ml instant coffee powder
Whipped cream for decorating (spoon into a piping bag with a rosette nozzle)
Chocolate sprinkles for decorating

Method

Make the Dark Chocolate Mousse – replace the brandy with whiskey.

Add the coffee powder to the melted chocolate – make sure that the coffee powder has melted before removing the chocolate mixture off the double boiler.

Spoon the chocolate mousse into the Irish coffee glasses.

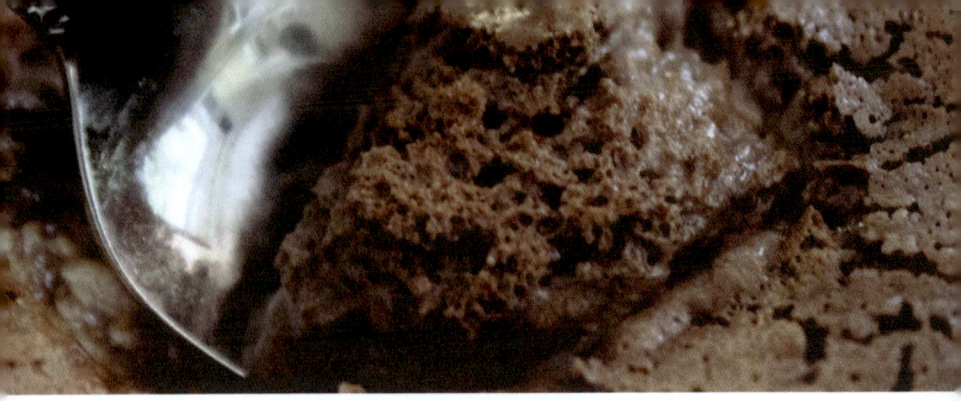

Irish Coffee Glass

Pipe the whipped cream on top of the chocolate mousse.

Decorate the cream with the chocolate sprinkles.

Kahlua Chocolate Mousse In Chocolate Shot Glasses

Serve Kahlua Chocolate Mousse – 1 per guest.

Ingredients

    White chocolate for making the shot glasses

    1 mixture of Basic Dark Chocolate Mousse

    50 ml Kahlua – substitute for the brandy

    Whipped cream for decorating (spoon into a piping bag with a rosette nozzle)

    Chocolate to make designs for decorating (melted)

Method

Melt the white chocolate in the top of a double boiler.

Pour the white chocolate into a shot glass mold such as the one picture below.

Shot Glass Mold

Leave the chocolate to set.

Remove the white chocolate shot glasses from the mold.

These shot glasses can be made a while before the time.

Make the Dark Chocolate Mousse – replace the brandy with Kahlua.

Chocolate Design To Decorate Chocolate Mousse

Spoon the chocolate mousse into a piping bag with a rosette nozzle.

Just before serving pipe the Kahlua chocolate mousse into the chocolate shot glasses.

Pipe rosettes of whipped cream on top of the chocolate mousse in the chocolate shot glasses.

Melt the chocolate and then drizzle the melted chocolate onto a pieced of parchment paper – see example below.

Leave the chocolate design to set.

Once the chocolate design has set, remove it from the parchment paper and decorate the chocolate mousse with the chocolate designs.

Peppermint Chocolate Mousse In Shot Glasses

Serve the Peppermint Chocolate Mousse – 1 per guest.

Ingredients

- 1 mixture of Basic Dark Chocolate Mousse
- 50 ml Peppermint Liqueur – substitute for the brandy
- Whipped cream for decorating (spoon into a piping bag with a rosette nozzle)
- Fresh peppermint leaves for decorating

Method

Make the Dark Chocolate Mousse – replace the brandy with Peppermint liqueur.

Spoon the chocolate mousse into a piping bag with a rosette nozzle.

Pipe the chocolate mousse into shot glasses.

Shot Glass

Pipe rosettes of whipped cream on top of the chocolate mousse in the shot glasses.

Decorate the chocolate mousse with fresh peppermint leaves.

Triple Chocolate Mousse Mini Cakes

Serve the Triple Chocolate Mousse Mini Cakes – 1 per guest.

Ingredients

- 400 g chocolate cookies (crushed)
- 75 ml butter (melted)
- 2 mixtures of Basic Dark Chocolate Mousse
- 600 g milk chocolate – substitute for dark chocolate
- 50 ml strong black coffee – substitute for the brandy
- 1 mixture of Basic White Chocolate Mousse
- Chocolate curls for decorating
- Icing sugar for dusting

Method

Combine the chocolate cookies and melted butter together.

Mix well.

Press the cookie mixture into the bottom of a greased spring-form pan (do not press the cookie crumbs around the sides of the pan).

Mini Spring-form Pans

Refrigerate the cookie bases in the spring-form pans for 10 minutes or until needed.

Now make the first Dark Chocolate Mousse mixture – no variations are required for the recipe.

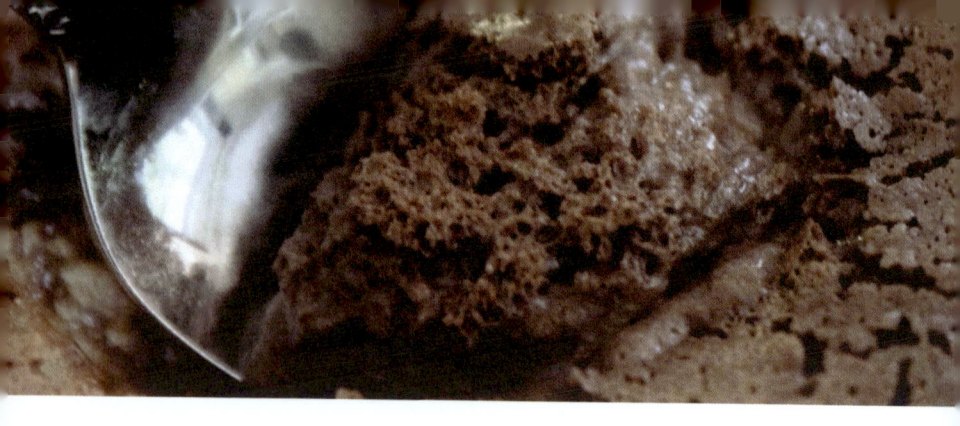

Divide the Dark Chocolate Mousse mixture into the spring-form pans on top of the cookie layer.

Make sure the layer is level and smooth on top.

Now make the second Dark Chocolate Mousse mixture – use milk chocolate instead of dark chocolate and use strong black coffee instead of brandy.

Gently spoon the Coffee Chocolate Mousse on top of the Dark Chocolate Mousse layer.

Make sure the layer is level and smooth on top.

Now make the White Chocolate Mousse mixture - no variations are required for the recipe.

Gently spoon the White Chocolate Mousse on top of the Coffee Chocolate Mousse layer.

Make sure the layer is level and smooth on top.

Refrigerate the mousse cakes for at least 6 hours to make sure they have set (preferably overnight).

Just before serving remove the chocolate mousse cakes from the spring-form pans.

Place each individual chocolate mousse cake into a glass dessert bowl.

Glass Dessert Bowl

Dust the individual mousse cakes with icing sugar.

Decorate the mousse cakes with chocolate curls.

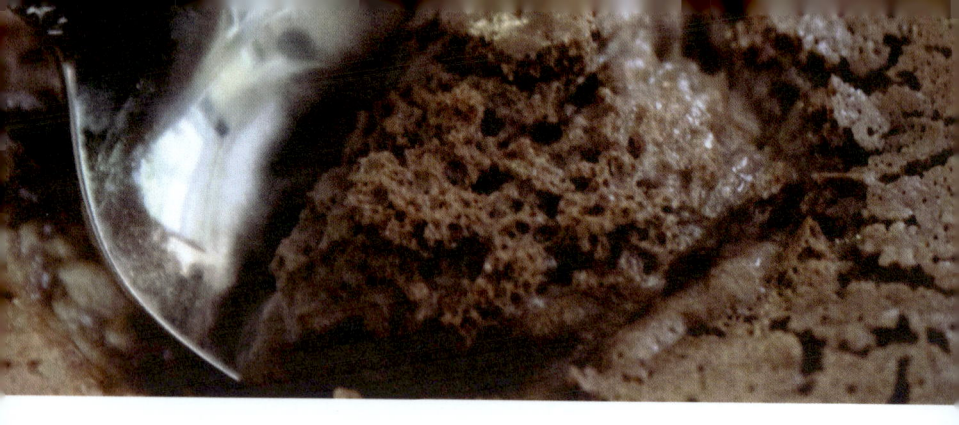

White Chocolate Mousse In Chocolate Sugar Cone Bowls

Serve the White Chocolate Mousse in Chocolate Sugar Cone Bowls – 1 per guest. This mousse recipe serves 4 servings.

Ingredients

- 3 eggs
- 375 ml flour
- 45 ml sugar
- 45 ml cocoa powder
- 45 ml oil
- 455 ml milk
- 1 mixture of Basic White Chocolate Mousse
- 10 ml strawberry extract – substitute for vanilla extract
- Few drops pink food coloring
- Whipped cream for decorating (place in a piping bag with a rosette nozzle)
- Whole fresh strawberries (hulled) for decorating

Method

Combine the eggs, flour, sugar, cocoa powder, oil and milk together.

Blend well.

Leave the mixture for 60 minutes.

Pour just enough batter into a greased hot pan to cover the bottom of the pan when the pan is tipped. Make the pancakes fairly thin.

When the edges of the pancake are lightly browned turn the pancake and cook on second side.

One the pancakes are all baked, use a large round cookie cutter to cut out circles in the pancakes.

Place the pancake circles into greased muffins pans.

Bake at 18 degrees C for 12 minutes.

Remove from the oven.

Remove from the muffin pans and cool on a wire rack.

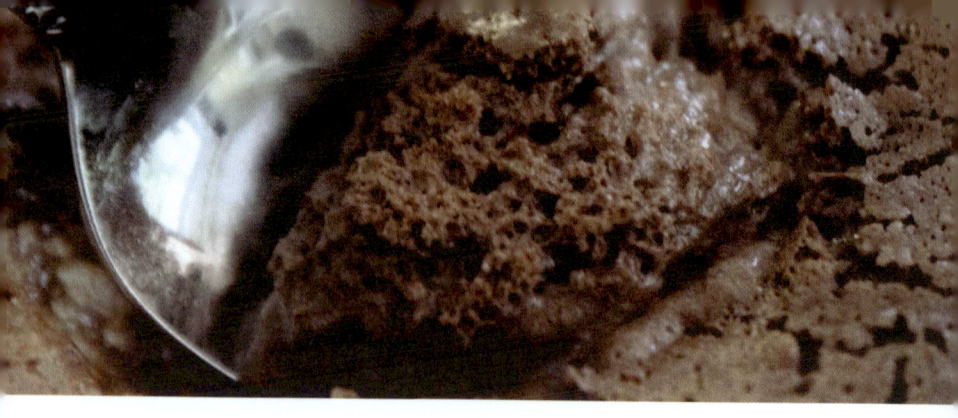

Now make the White Chocolate Mousse mixture – replace the vanilla extract with strawberry extract.

Add a few drops of pink food coloring.

Just before serving spoon the White Chocolate Mousse into the Chocolate Sugar Cone Bowls.

Pipe whipped cream rosettes on top of the white chocolate mousse.

Decorate with the whole strawberries.

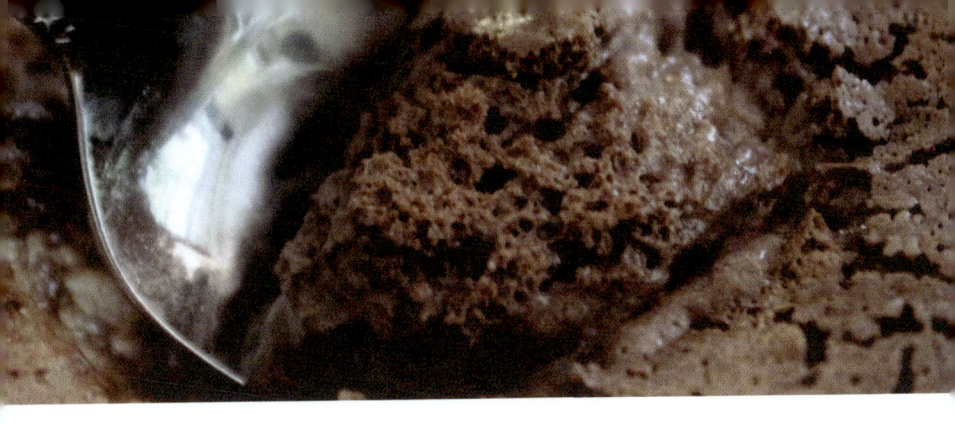

White Chocolate Mousse In Dark Chocolate Bowls

Serve the White Chocolate Mousse in Dark Chocolate Bowls – 1 per guest. This mousse recipe serves 4 servings.

Ingredients

- Dark chocolate (to make chocolate bowls)
- Balloons (to make chocolate bowls)
- 1 mixture of Basic White Chocolate Mousse
- Whipped cream for decorating (place in a piping bag with a rosette nozzle)
- Chocolate curls for decorating

Method

You can make the chocolate bowls a few days before the time.

Blow the balloons up and tie them closed.

Melt the chocolate in the top of a double boiler.

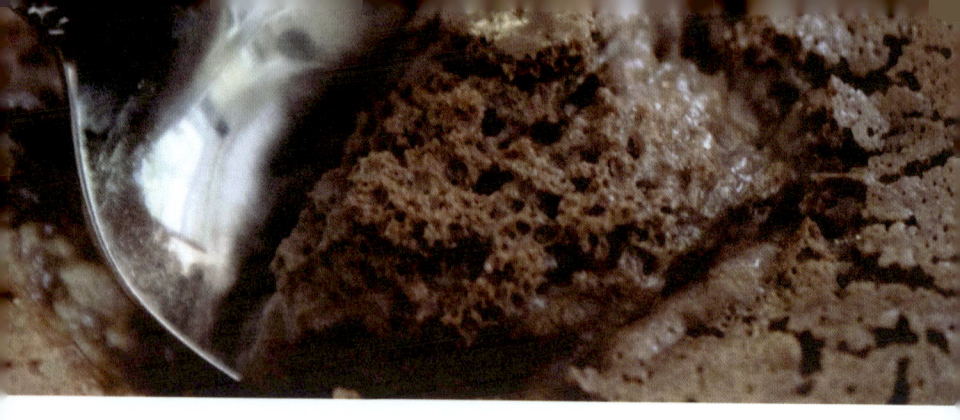

Stir well to make sure that the chocolate is smooth.

Hold the balloon by the knot and dip the balloon into the melted chocolate.

Dip the balloon as deep as you want the bowl to be.

Make sure that the balloon is dipped evenly in the chocolate as there shouldn't be any "holes" in the bowl.

Place the dipped balloons on a baking sheet covered with parchment paper.

Allow the chocolate to harden at room temperature.

To remove the balloons from the chocolate bowl, press the sides of the balloon to release it from the chocolate.

Press your finger onto the balloon and make a small slit in the balloon above your finger. Allow the air to escape while regulating it with your finger.

Pull the balloon away from the chocolate.

The chocolate bowl will need to be stored in a cool place if you are making them well ahead of time.

Now make the White Chocolate Mousse mixture - no variations are required for the recipe.

Just before serving spoon the White Chocolate Mousse into the dark chocolate bowls.

Pipe rosettes of whipped cream on top of the chocolate mousse.

Decorate with the chocolate curls.

CHOCOLATE MOUSSE

SOUFFLÉS

Dessert Soufflés

Tips For Baking Soufflés

Make sure that the egg whites have been beaten to the right consistency - do not over beat (the whites will appear dry and granular if they are over beaten).

Do not over bake the soufflés, press a skewer into the soufflé. If it does not come out clean, continue baking the soufflé for 2 or 3 minutes.

The exterior of the soufflé should be set while the centre of the soufflé should be slightly loose when shaken. The soufflé should have risen above the dish.

Grease the ramekins with butter.

To help the soufflés rise properly, run your finger around the rim of the ramekins to wipe the edges clean.

Serve the soufflés immediately after removing them from the oven.

When folding the whisked egg whites into the egg mixture – first fold a ¼ of the whisked egg whites into cooled egg mixture to lighten it. Then fold in the remaining whites. Do this very gently. Use a rubber spatula and fold just until the egg whites are incorporated. Do not over mix the mixture or it will fall flat.

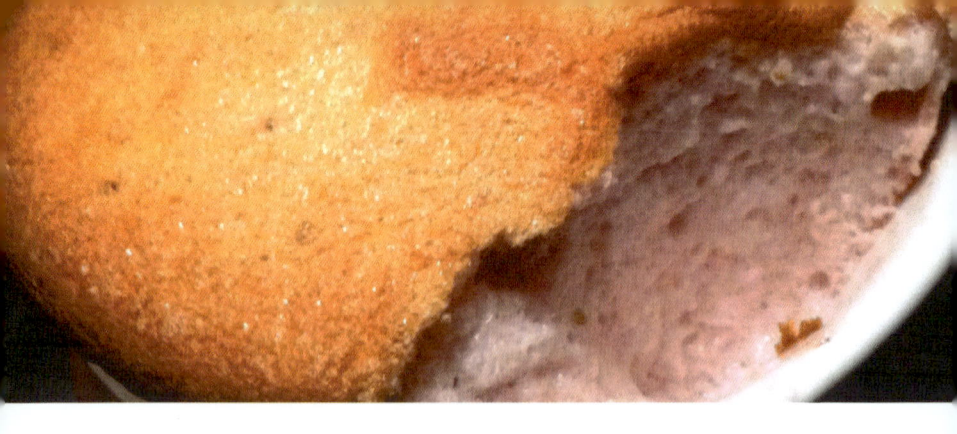

Chocolate Soufflé Recipe

Ingredients

- 120 g dark chocolate (get the best quality chocolate you can afford)
- 100 ml thick cream
- 2 egg yolks
- 4 egg whites
- 50 g caster sugar
- 80 g dark chocolate
- 50 ml thick cream
- Whipped cream for decorating (place in a piping bag with a rosette nozzle)
- Chocolate curls for decorating

Method

Break the chocolate into small pieces.

Combine the chocolate pieces and thick cream together in the top of a double boiler.

Stir until the chocolate has melted.

Remove from the heat.

Add the egg yolks and mix well.

Whisk the egg whites until frothy.

Gradually add the sugar.

Whisk until stiff peaks form.

Fold the egg whites into the chocolate mixture (do not over mix).

Pour the mixture into 4 ramekins greased with butter.

Bake at 150 degrees C for 30 minutes.

While the soufflés are baking combine the chocolate and the thick cream together in the top of a double boiler.

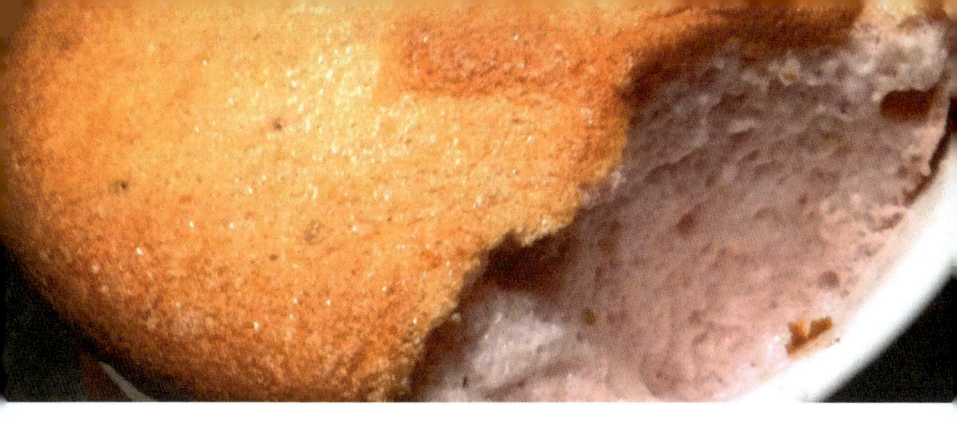

Stir until the chocolate has melted.

Remove from the heat.

Remove the soufflés from the oven.

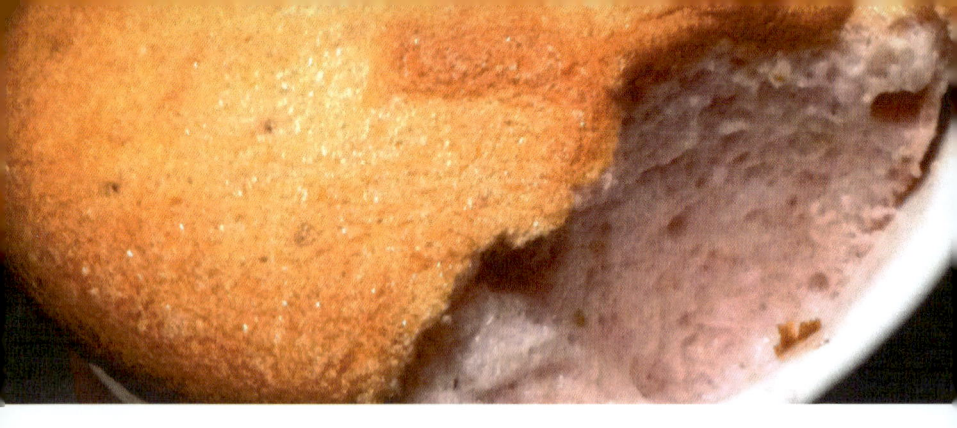

Make a hole in the centre of each soufflé and pour the melted chocolate into the hole in each soufflé.

Pipe rosettes of whipped cream on top of the chocolate soufflés.

Decorate the chocolate soufflés with chocolate curls.

Serve immediately.

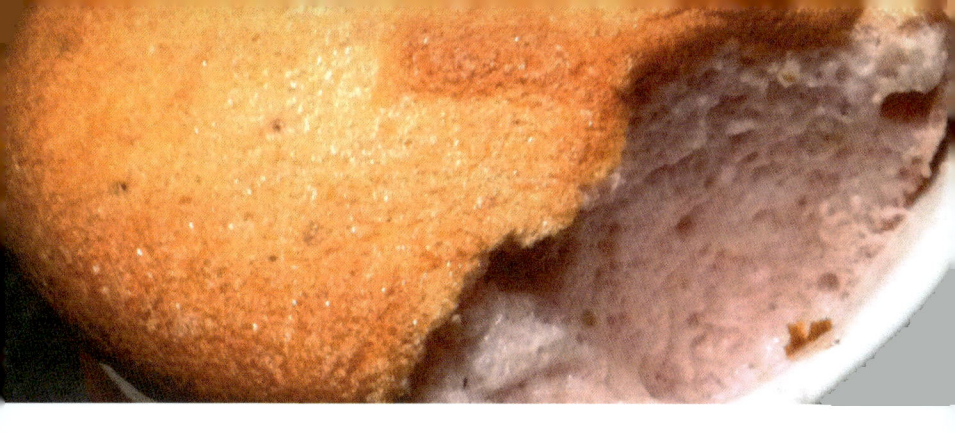

Chocolate Raspberry Soufflé

Ingredients

- 500 ml raspberries
- 12,5 ml caster sugar
- 12,5 ml Muscovado sugar
- Water to cover the fruit halfway up in the saucepan
- 2 whole cloves
- 1 cinnamon stick
- 120 g dark chocolate (get the best quality chocolate you can afford)
- 100 ml thick cream
- 2 egg yolks
- 4 egg whites
- 50 g caster sugar
- 80 g dark chocolate
- 50 ml thick cream
- Whipped cream for serving

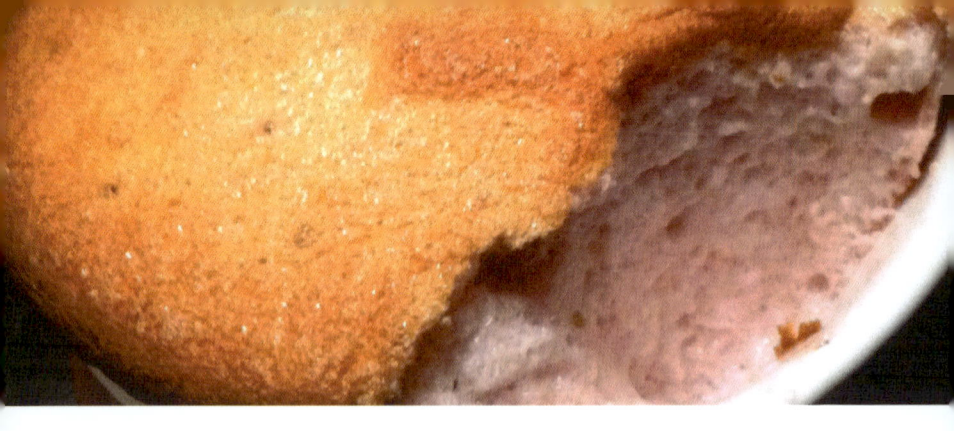

Method

Combine the raspberries, castor sugar and Muscovado sugar together in a saucepan.

Add the water, cloves and cinnamon sticks.

Bring to a boil.

Cover the saucepan with a lid and reduce the heat.

Simmer for 7 minutes.

Remove from the heat and keep warm.

Break the chocolate into small pieces.

Combine the chocolate pieces and thick cream together in the top of a double boiler.

Stir until the chocolate has melted.

Remove from the heat.

Add the egg yolks and mix well.

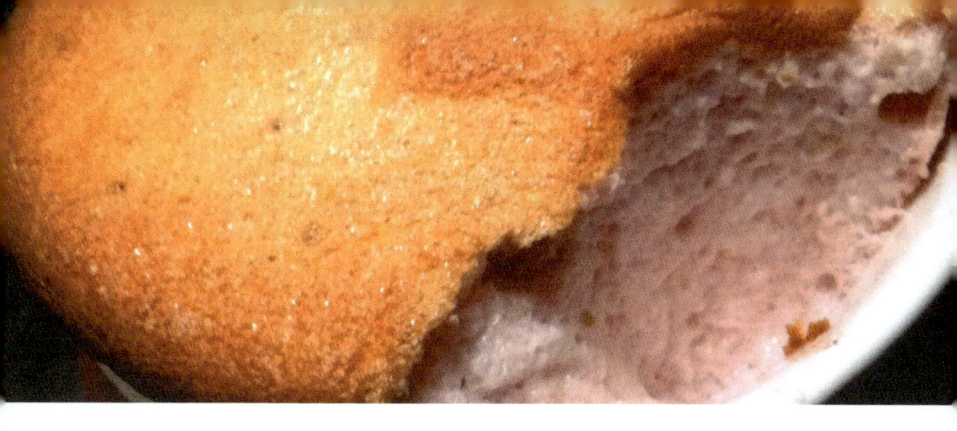

Whisk the egg whites until frothy.

Gradually add the sugar.

Whisk until stiff peaks form.

Fold the egg whites into the chocolate mixture (do not over mix).

Pour the mixture into 4 ramekins greased with butter.

Bake at 150 degrees C for 30 minutes.

While the soufflés are baking combine the chocolate and the thick cream together in the top of a double boiler.

Stir until the chocolate has melted.

Remove from the heat.

Remove the soufflés from the oven.

Make a hole in the centre of each soufflé and pour the melted chocolate into the hole in each soufflé.

Serve the soufflés immediately with the raspberry compote and whipped cream.

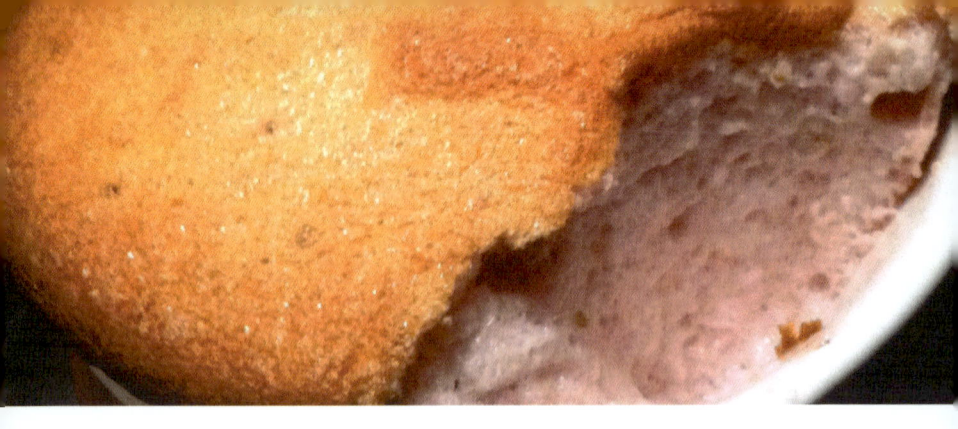

Lemon Soufflé

Ingredients

- 187 ml milk
- 7,5 ml lemon zest
- 187 ml sugar
- 3 egg yolks
- 37,5 ml flour
- 93 ml lemon juice
- 3 ml salt
- 4 large egg whites
- 3 ml cream of tartar
- Icing sugar to dust soufflés
- Blueberry compote

Method

Scald the milk and lemon zest together.

Remove the milk mixture from the heat.

Leave the milk mixture to cool.

Whisk the sugar and egg yolks together until light and fluffy.

Add the flour to the egg mixture.

Blend well.

Combine the milk mixture and the egg mixture together.

Mix well.

Add the lemon juice and salt.

Place the mixture in the top of a double boiler and cook until the mixture is thick and creamy.

Remove the mixture from the heat.

Leave the mixture to cool completely.

Whisk the egg whites and cream of tartar together until soft peaks form.

Fold the egg whites and the lemon mixture together.

Do not over mix the mixture.

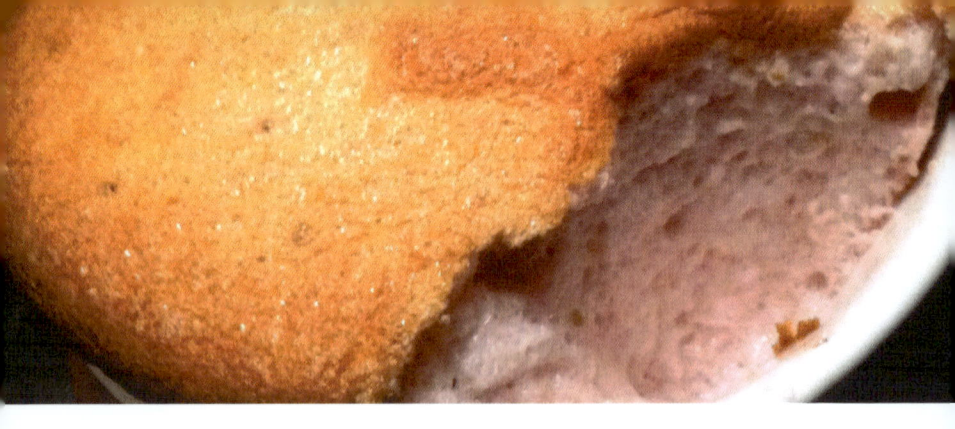

Pour the mixture into greased ramekins.

Bake at 400 degrees F for 10 minutes.

Reduce the heat to 350 degrees F.

Bake for 5 minutes.

Remove the soufflés from the oven.

Dust the soufflés with icing sugar.

Serve immediately with the blueberry compote.

Lime And Coconut Soufflé

Ingredients

- 187 ml coconut milk
- 7,5 ml lime zest
- 187 ml sugar
- 3 egg yolks
- 37,5 ml flour
- 93 ml lime juice
- 3 ml salt
- 4 large egg whites
- 3 ml cream of tartar
- Icing sugar to dust soufflés

Method

Scald the coconut milk and lime zest together.

Remove the coconut milk mixture from the heat.

Leave the coconut milk mixture to cool.

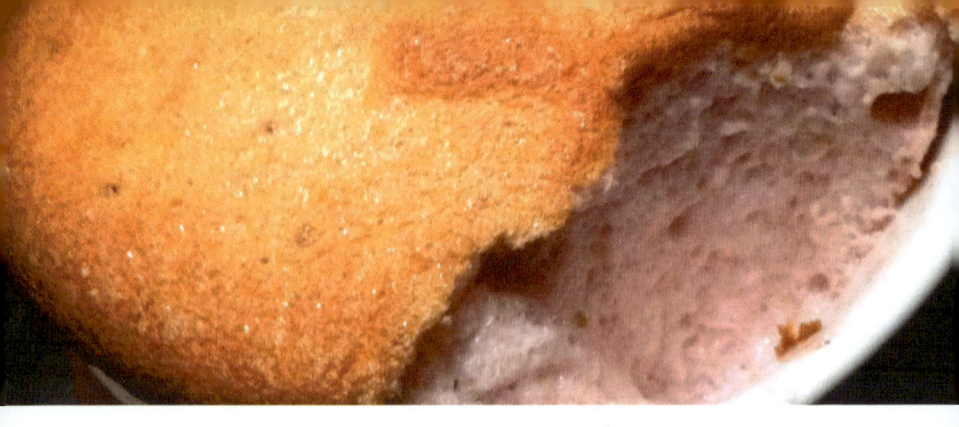

Whisk the sugar and egg yolks together until light and fluffy.

Add the flour to the egg mixture.

Blend well.

Combine the coconut milk mixture and the egg mixture together.

Mix well.

Add the lime juice and salt.

Place the mixture in the top of a double boiler and cook until the mixture is thick and creamy.

Remove the mixture from the heat.

Leave the mixture to cool completely.

Whisk the egg whites and cream of tartar together until soft peaks form.

Fold the egg whites and the lemon mixture together.

Do not over mix the mixture.

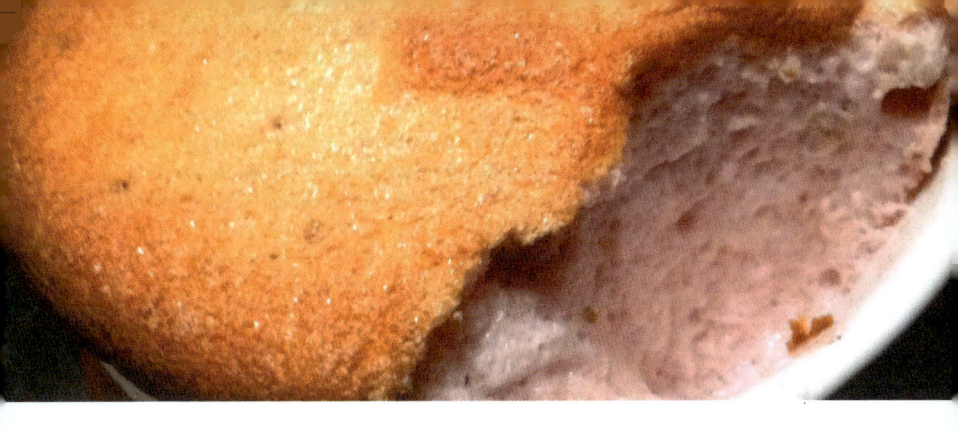

Pour the mixture into greased ramekins.

Bake at 400 degrees F for 10 minutes.

Reduce the heat to 350 degrees F.

Bake for 5 minutes.

Remove the soufflés from the oven.

Dust the soufflés with icing sugar.

Serve immediately.

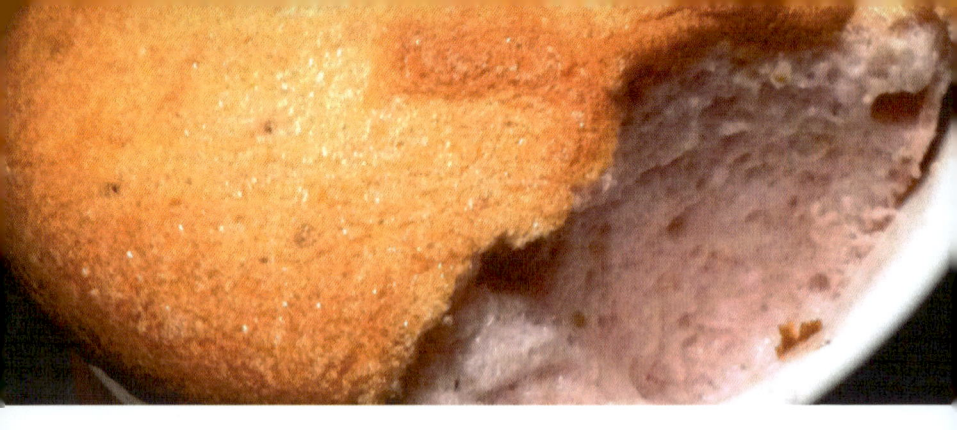

Mocha Soufflé

Ingredients

- 120 g dark chocolate (get the best quality chocolate you can afford)
- 10 ml instant coffee powder
- 100 ml thick cream
- 2 egg yolks
- 4 egg whites
- 50 g caster sugar
- 50 ml Kahlua
- 50 ml thick cream
- Icing sugar to dust soufflés

Method

Break the chocolate into small pieces.

Combine the chocolate pieces, instant coffee powder and thick cream together in the top of a double boiler.

Stir until the chocolate has melted.

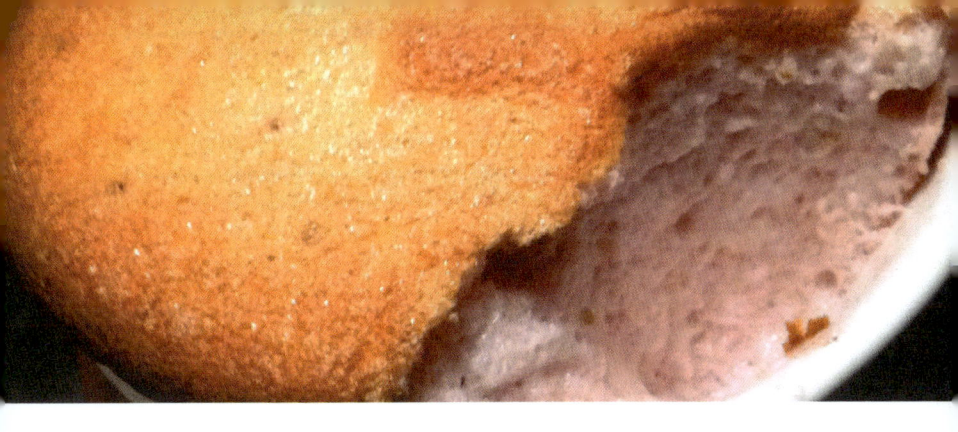

Remove from the heat.

Add the egg yolks and mix well.

Whisk the egg whites until frothy.

Gradually add the sugar.

Whisk until stiff peaks form.

Fold the egg whites into the chocolate mixture (do not over mix).

Pour the mixture into 4 ramekins greased with butter.

Bake at 150 degrees C for 30 minutes.

While the soufflés are baking combine the Kahlua and thick cream together. Mix well.

Remove the soufflés from the oven.

Make a hole in the centre of each soufflé and pour the Kahlua into the hole in each soufflé.

Dust the soufflés with icing sugar. Serve immediately.

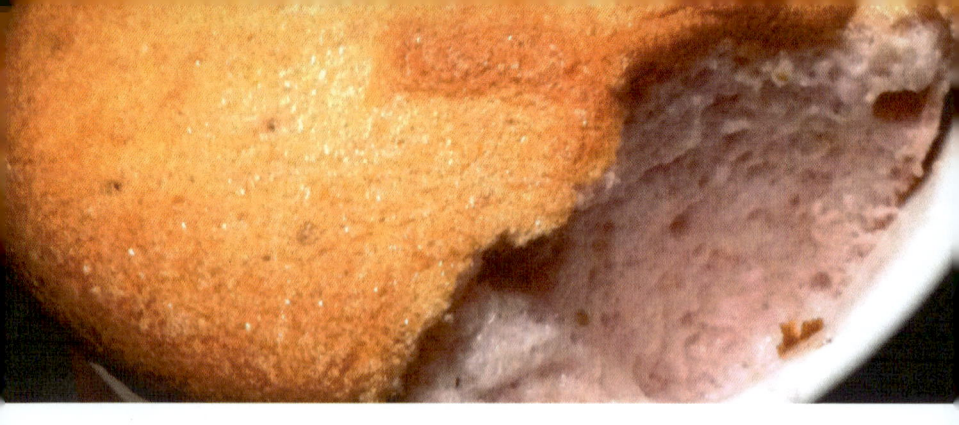

Rose Soufflé

Ingredients

- 120 g white chocolate (get the best quality chocolate you can afford)
- 100 ml thick cream
- 10 ml rose water
- 2 egg yolks
- 4 egg whites
- 50 g caster sugar
- 80 g white chocolate
- 50 ml thick cream
- Icing sugar for dusting soufflés
- Rose petals for decorating

Method

Break the white chocolate into small pieces.

Combine the white chocolate pieces and thick cream together in the top of a double boiler.

Stir until the white chocolate has melted.

Remove from the heat.

Mix in the rose water.

Add the egg yolks and mix well.

Whisk the egg whites until frothy.

Gradually add the sugar.

Whisk until stiff peaks form.

Fold the egg whites into the chocolate mixture (do not over mix).

Pour the mixture into 4 ramekins greased with butter.

Bake at 150 degrees C for 30 minutes.

While the soufflés are baking combine the chocolate and the thick cream together in the top of a double boiler.

Stir until the chocolate has melted.

Remove from the heat.

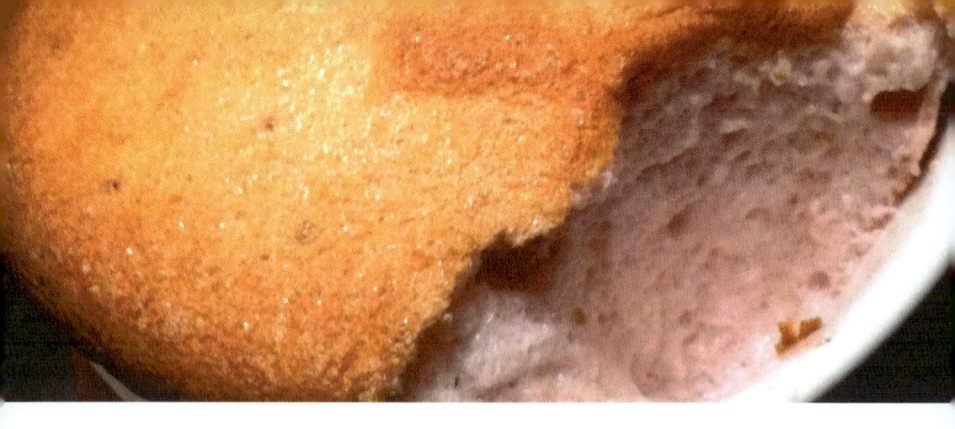

Remove the soufflés from the oven.

Make a hole in the centre of each soufflé and pour the melted chocolate into the hole in each soufflé.

Dust with icing sugar.

Decorate with the rose petals.

Serve immediately.

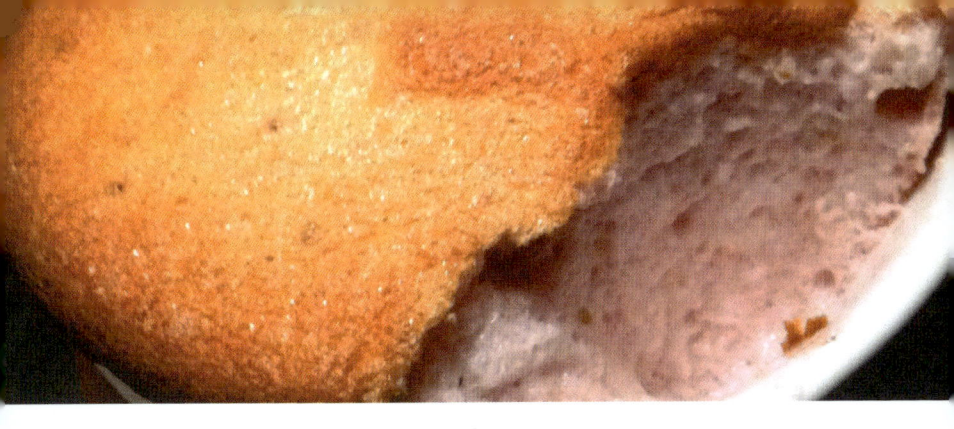

Vanilla Soufflé

Ingredients

- 120 g milk chocolate (get the best quality chocolate you can afford)
- 100 ml thick cream
- 10 ml vanilla extract
- 2 egg yolks
- 4 egg whites
- 50 g caster sugar
- 80 g milk chocolate
- 50 ml thick cream
- Icing sugar for dusting soufflés

Method

Break the milk chocolate into small pieces.

Combine the milk chocolate pieces and thick cream together in the top of a double boiler.

Stir until the milk chocolate has melted.

Remove from the heat.

Mix in the vanilla extract.

Add the egg yolks and mix well.

Whisk the egg whites until frothy.

Gradually add the sugar.

Whisk until stiff peaks form.

Fold the egg whites into the chocolate mixture (do not over mix).

Pour the mixture into 4 ramekins greased with butter.

Bake at 150 degrees C for 30 minutes.

While the soufflés are baking combine the milk chocolate and the thick cream together in the top of a double boiler.

Stir until the milk chocolate has melted.

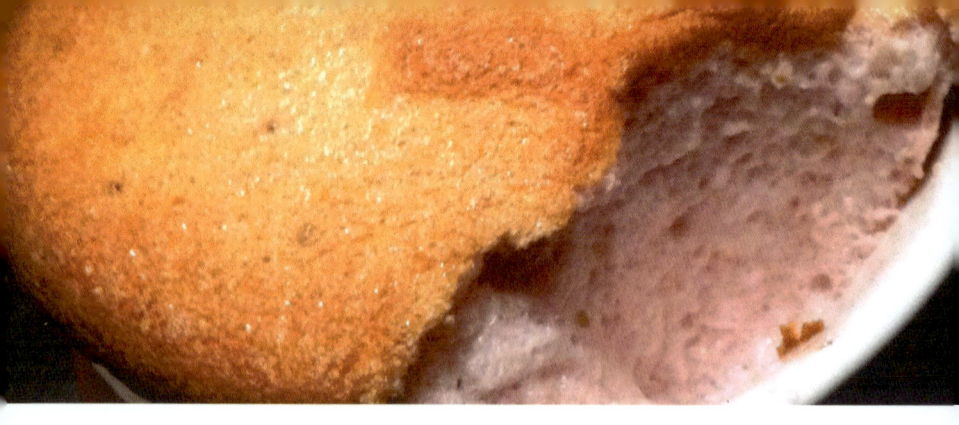

Remove from the heat.

Remove the soufflés from the oven.

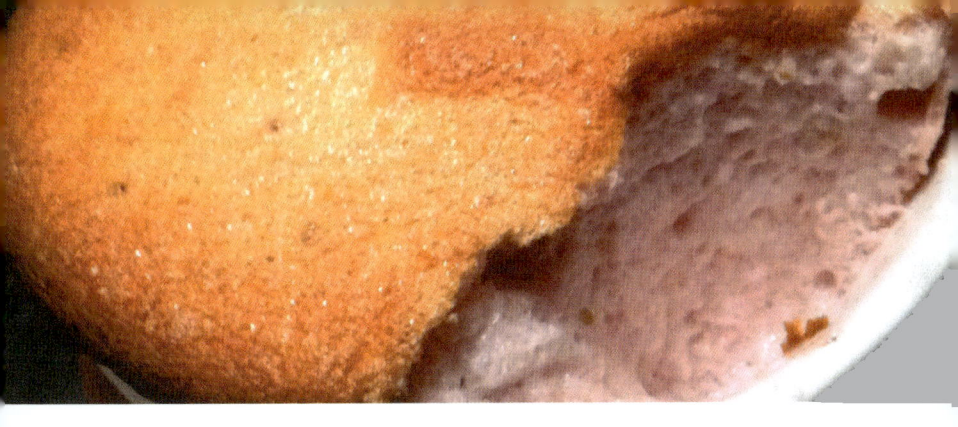

Make a hole in the centre of each soufflé and pour the melted milk chocolate mixture into the hole in each soufflé.

Dust with icing sugar.

Serve immediately.

Printed in Great Britain
by Amazon